Three White Horses

Three White Horses
Still Lifes

Jonas Zdanys
poems

Sou Vai Keng
paintings

LITERARY PRESS
LAMAR UNIVERSITY

ISBN: 978-1-942956-43-3
Library of Congress Control Number: 2017946564

Acknowledgments
Poems 7, 14, and 16 appeared originally in *all roads will
lead you home* and poems 11, 13, 21, and 37 appeared
originally in *The Galway Review*. I am grateful to Sacred
Heart University for granting me time to work on this
collection and on other volumes.

Book design by Regina Schroeder

Manufactured in the United States of America

Lamar University Literary Press
Beaumont, Texas

for my mother

Poetry from Lamar University Literary Press

Erin Murphy, *Ancilla*
Laurence Musgrove, *Local Bird*
Dave Oliphant, *The Pilgrimage, Selected Poems: 1962-2012*
Kornelijus Platelis, *Solitary Architectures*
Carol Coffee Reposa, *Underground Musicians*
Jan Seale, *The Parkinson Poems*
Steven Schroeder, *the moon, not the finger, pointing*
Carol Smallwood, *Water, Earth, Air, Fire, and Picket Fences*
Glen Sorestad, *Hazards of Eden*
W.K. Stratton, *Ranchero Ford / Dying in Red Dirt Country*
Wally Swist, *Invocation*
Jonas Zdanys (ed.), *Pushing the Envelope, Epistolary Poems*
Jonas Zdanys, *Red Stones*

For information on these and other
Lamar University Literary Press books go to
www.Lamar.edu/literarypress

Selected Books by Jonas Zdanys

Poems in English

St. Brigid's Well. 2017
Red Stones. 2016
Cormorants. 2013
The Kingfisher's Reign. 2012
The Thin Light of Winter. 2009
Salt. 2007
The Woman on the Bridge. 2005
The White City. 2004
White. 2004
Lithuanian Crossing. 1999
Water Light. 1997
The White Bend of the River. 1994
The Metaphysics of Wolves. 1994
Maine Aubade. 1990
Voice on an Anthill. 1982.

Poems in English and Lithuanian

Two Voices/Du balsai. 2017
Preludes After Rain/Preliudai po lietaus. 2017

Poems in Lithuanian

Ikaro prisikėlimas. 2014
Tarpdury. 2008
Dūmų stulpai. 2002
Dotnuvos stoty. 1999
Aušros daina. 1993

Three white horses stir
trapped in the language
of the dead as light
empties like an oracle
across the blue
smoke of heaven.

— *St. Brigid's Well*

Poems

Paintings

queen of the night / frontis & cover

I.

The clock strikes midnight.
Night began like a last letter against
the cold, the flat light the color of shadows
and the shaken wings of cicadas drying
to dust and brown grass under the ice
as the world revolved and time passed
in brisk detachments down the road.
It had snowed all day, the sky fading
to brittle knots and lesser birds folding
to dark echoes on the streetlamps and trees.
When we came back, a haze of blue
smoke blinded the wall, the frail silence
of the street following up the long stairs.
Outside the window, past the red tiles
of the rooftops, in the old square near
the fountain, three white horses rounding
the circle turned and swelled in bronze.
They watched the strangers pass,
the secret given them by the world
an allegory of winter and love,
quick as their eyes could count
the lowest number on the wheel.
And the sky turned dark as a wilted rose,
black and brittle at the root.
And shadows leaked unfocused
at the center and the edge.

2.

Your skin tasted like the air along
the river, bitter and quick, one light
shining in the window of the house
beyond the bend of the road.
The silence of God muddled the trees
as the heavens closed and reconciled
with light, and the twelve winds
survived the dream's last hour.
In the distance, rising and falling,
the echoes of stars scratched effigies
on broken stone, gatherings of lost birds
patched breathless near the outer gate.
Clouds of snow spun clockwise
in the timeless glass of heaven
and earth, and the dry bones rode
on clear wings to history and dust.
Wait. None of this may be right.
Tonight memory twists and turns
in a drunken room, passion ending
in the echoes of birds in locked boxes
as the vestments of glass struggle and dull.
The course of the world slips away and
the year loses its footing in the street.
The speculations of what is true conclude
without conviction or success, the points
of the wind rose rusted in the arches.
Consolations of the past darken
to bottomless reductions in the mirror,
the artificial line with no fixed point
compounded at the margins as they fall.
The synthesis of fire and ice drones
in the hollows, wings the white wall.

3.

I watched you standing in the hallway,
red shoes nervous in your hand,
a gray shape of soot and stone in a
silent corner of the night leaning against
the wall like an impossible dream.
Footsteps shake the floor, the secret out,
and the city slides into its own blue light.
The long burdens and spare parts
of this place as the great wheel spins
its last come and go as they will.
The day will not reconcile with night,
peels the muster of the rounding stair.
Things sleep in the tarnish of ice,
cold in a cold world where time
wears out, and the street that leads
home darkens on its steep ascent.
Its shadows tilt the shadows back
in a long-abandoned room.

4.

Try to remember the way
the dark bridge above the dark river
stands against the white of winter,
the way dust coats the thin edges
of the window blinds in the old room,
the way smoke from the low chimneys
in the narrow alley dissolves slowly
in the air, the way the thin street
turns back to the house, filled
with memory and desire, and the sky
erupts with the sound of lost birds
in a warp of November snow.
Truth springs up, heavy with the
passing years, like a mirror
in an empty house that shatters
against a sudden wall.
Take it all in as the year sets low
on a horizon of cut stone, follow
the shapes and signs that lift
the secrets of another life.
Clip the unexpected.
Catch the one who was the first to fall.
It may be enough.
You may remember the way
the moon wanes across the corners
of the house, bleeding away like
a thousand wings, the way
the barrier of dead roots covets
the new world, locked in the tempo
of shift and change, the way
light sinks into an open door
near the edge of the infinite road
and follows, follows, follows.

5.

Nothing will happen.
The single stem of a cold night
will break like a blue vein,
the windows and doors of gray
towns claiming no further warrants.
A brittle snow will bring November
to a close and the trees along
the river in the center of the city
will thin to slow brick walls, crossed
thresholds, the disorder that sinks
to other shapes in a changing sky.
The old gods, carved in runes and
dry timbers, will cave the darkening
shadows of the streets.
The indifference of time will slide
to its quick, a black angel floating
in dark water under an old stone bridge.
Near the yards, the pulse of rolled
steel will deafen the light and air.
Memory, charred in its own dry visions,
will walk out the door into a silver light.
Nothing will gather into nothing.

6.

The faces in the shop windows
grow old in the same country,
turn gray on the same cross streets,
rise and fall in the same small corners.
It is growing cold a mile down the road,
trains stop, death comes hobbling
like a strange dog suddenly at the door.
The sky beyond opens as if created for the
first time, filled with pale flowers, and a red
bird lifts slowly across the dark steel rails.
An old man's hand works the folds
of the empty wall in the dark, midnight
coiling along the bricks in the walk.
Something light and dry touches his face,
ripples and blurs in dead glass.
The next moment falters, then the next.

7.

I live simply, raise no alarms.
Darkness flows around itself
as eyes stare past the green walls
and light glances off the single vase
in the center of the table
that holds no stems or flowers.
Night deepens without commotion,
tilts its roots into the room,
the world in sleep and second sight.
The table is covered with the heads
of matches, carefully arranged
in circles and lines, a dangerous plain
near the closed attic door.
I endure the shift of things,
watch a small brown spider
make its way among the
phosphorus stones, quicker
than a human hand, my fingers
tapping on the table's edge.
It is centered on its spot,
threading through the rows
of matchheads as if some
needle's eye or frightened wish.
Wind rattles the window glass,
blessing the ground
and surviving the ice.
I stay up half the night
awake in every nerve,
the promise of conflagration
in the dusted air.
The great wheel spins.
A match scratches across
the coarse plate, circles
aimlessly for a minute
in the streak of its pursuit.

The spider dances for
redemption on the table
among the yellow flames.
My fingers tap the edge in time,
nourished on tears and smoke.

8.

Truth tastes like ashes in my mouth
as I sit in the deep gray light.
The rust on the posts of the green
bridge unwinds the clocks, cold-eyed
in the water of the brown river that
floods across a dry arrangement
of stunned voices. I walk from room
to room listening. The hard rattle
of night spins on its own black edge.
The shade on the window thumps
like the white flame of a lost love.
Outside, whistles running in the streets
call the raw dogs. It's no use complaining:
these are all clear sounds. Only time
is a ghost whose lips are perpetually
sealed until the bone of chaos scratches
the word and the circles of heaven break.
Beyond the window, where the flats
brook the ridge, it comes to a dead rest.

9.

When all else whitens on the roofs,
when wayward things come home
to roost to a new red deep in iron
and stone and the day staggers to
a brawl in the dying street, the years
howling through the light at the edge
of a breathless universe –
you know there is no way to go
but back, to dream in the dead
of night of insistent voices in the dark,
the forgotten places behind closed
doors, the way all lovers move and
pass, hair smooth and loose, in all
the corners of all the rooms of this city.
And then a deeper sleep, so many endings
out beyond the opening gates, the sound
of running horses as the scroll unwinds.
The soul, tangled in its own patterns,
cannot see tomorrow unfold, cannot
lurch headlong into its passive voice.
The night is forever cold and struck
and everything is under siege.

10.

In late November, the hours
turn brittle and dull
as reason and forgotten truth
drive the agitated form.
The days pass with eyes cast down,
things turning inside out
and the ground settling
to black frost as the wind lifts
to thresholds and ash.
Someone throws the first stone,
weeping for the life he's lived,
and old men search
the backyards for their own graves
as light mires the vulnerable air.
It is growing cold and the sky blows
to winter, humpbacked and long.
Life hangs by a thread
in empty windows.
Behind the red door, my hand
in the soft hollow of your back,
we stand pressed together
fumbling in a dark we know
will not come again.
My heart rises like a shout.
The night is a long excuse.
Love is a dark cut
on a wooden frame.
I close my eyes and
think of morning.
May it not be so.
May it not be so.

II.

Midnight kneels in the park
by the river like a blind child.
No one can hear or see
and the light that comes
unexpectedly around the corner
is black at the core.
It drifts in its own darkness,
scattering to shudders
on the windows and ledges
of slow gray houses, remnants
of voices on a rising wind.
The secrets of the street
whisper across the thin cut
of the moon, clouds brushing
invisible through the dust
of the rooftops and walls.
Ghosts loiter on stone benches.
Cold crouches in the passing bell.
The mute white horse sleeps
with eyes open, swept free and frail
in the refuge of dead branches,
one of the shapes of the world
that cast no shadows in the glass.
Its sad bones land soft
and low on the dark street.

12.

The streetlamp casts black shadows
across the curtains that float
to the middle of the floor
and darken the room.
The earth turns toward dawn,
the wind out of the east.
The grief of the unanswerable
question spreads over the walls
like a hard inscription
and the snow drifts down.
Cold owls gather white ice
as the hour passes, time
the mute timber of a sallow light.
The ghost of her blind father
is home again: the white shadow
rising above the black street
after a long wandering,
the last grain of sand in his eye.
The weight of things falls to its end:
the world is a hollow sphere,
the last circle, filled with illusions
of smoke where spiders in the
corners of lost rooms mumble
and weave and the deep of night
cannot shake itself awake.

13.

The shapes reflected
in the high windows
erode in the snow, lights
moving through the backyards
in bewildered echoes, dying
twice on the stained wood floor.
It is the thing that is important,
seeing with open eyes beyond
the mind's eye, the new day
driven through the gate
even when the dark is too deep.
Tomorrow will die by your
hand, the end not yet written,
and the war will end.
The mirror mocks the sky's
decline, ticking like a clock.

14.

You dream of a long hall, dimly lit,
where breaths flutter against dark walls,
a white moth drumming on a hanging bulb;
of a quiet old room with green carpets,
a barefoot woman anxious with love
stretched on a hard brown chair;
of an empty bed at the end of winter,
a black skirt laced with fine stitches
draped loosely on a faded rail;
of arms and thighs wrapped together
in secret, faces pressing tense on a rug's
frayed edge, reflected in the pane;
of yourself, dry as salt in flutters of air,
floating through the ends of a bitter
earth and watching, watching.
These shadows mock the thin
disorder of the night, the paradox
of the zero and the one.

15.

The slow breath of a lost horse
standing alone in the snow
at midnight in winter wakes
the seed asleep in the cold ground.
He leaves no tracks as the earth
comes up out of darkness and moves
slowly toward a tenuous light.
The shape of the sky is constant,
the wound on his leg dark wood that
palls to yellow and stifles with blood.
Black cinders of houses burning
to dust beyond the fences spread
across a world that will never end
and the patience of desire endures
as it grapples for hours and fades.
That truth is always bitter in its own
defeat, no matter the threshold or the
sad impermanence of white stars.
The snow for now has stopped.
The radiance of things loses its place.
The uncontrollable season prods the year.
The horse suddenly shakes his head,
the sound of his mane and slow breathing
in the shallows of the trees an unexpected
comfort to the living and the dead.

16.

A small vine of light crawls
across the floor and snow freezes
on the window overhead, a needle
of ice forever pointing northward.
The old man leaning against
the wall reaches for the soft edge
of the universe or the mercies of time
that transfix the unmade bed.
He knows both will come when
the sun at last rises, cut loose for
a hundred years in the narrow streets,
the scar of a sad truth troubling
the careless door, but desires neither.
He'd rather hold the moon in his
hand as it sinks into its own light,
live forever in the soft rattle of summer
flowers, in a life that is not his alone.
But he knows, he knows, and turns his head.
The few stars that remain fuse to
stained glass in the upstairs room.
Shadows whisper of a kindness that may
come in the end, implacable and white.

17.

The history of this place concedes
nothing as things turn inside out,
infinite and dim, and the constellations
drift down along the red brick walls
and the moon slowly runs out of air:
the last thing we think about
when dreams of journeys bend
like wet grass in running water
and the field in the end is lost.
Hands call back the sky, a distant
sound steadies the eye that bears
witness on a windless day.
The years like black rock roll away,
stretch across the line of roofs
where everything is now,
where the day peels to its own negative
and is locked in a small black box.
They radiate in lines in every direction,
each a pain I no longer want to know.
I dream of love and lost cities,
turn my face to the icing river,
to the darkness, the silence, the wind.

18.

There is a point where eternity
opens, scrawled against the low
horizon in late fall, and love
is heavy in thin white branches.
The world often brings regret
and remains a semblance of light
drifting through an empty sky,
a threnody of mirrors and birds.
Above the bed the wheel unwinds
taking the hour by surprise, standing
still and moving all at once.
The ceremony of time anoints
its own indifference, the blade
of a knife keeping court in a dark wall.
Morning will bring a dream
of summer houses and sad songs,
wild flowers pressed against a face
in the pleasures of another dawn.
I close my eyes and wait.

19.

Sleep overcomes us both,
the empty gesture of redemption
leaving no mark.
You arch your back,
your skin white as winter,
a dream divided against the moon.
The world has taken us over,
exchanging the promise of form
for the breach of shadow.
I did not want to live like this,
the occasions of night improperly
rendered, a gray person dressed
in gray pressed on a hard gray floor.
I could be God, spreading
my wings, flying wherever I want,
navigating the maze even
with eyes closed, drifting safely
to the south along the brown river.
This was a thought I thought many
years ago but have since forgotten,
the confusions of invisible things
racing across the ceiling
with the flickerings of snow
as the light falls and falls.
I fall into the burden of these images,
close myself away from the world
and meet the universe at its rim:
tonight is a stopped clock, a short
red truth that frets its hour, and I am
on the wrong side of the wall.

20.

The carved lines of ice on the window
mean nothing as they dry to the coarse
powder of infinity. There is no obligation,
no period of the moon that frames
grand dreams and blinds the sky to ruin
and void. I stare on, the slate of the future
in the hieroglyphs in the window
useless as the blade of a dull knife.
How do we snare our lives together,
the city at rope's end, how do we enter
again into a late dim light as the world
no longer grinds its firm edges?
How do you choose yourself as the earth
bows to an empty mission and strains
against the hull's black plates? How?
The silence of the unbroken night
has sunk into its past, time in slow descent,
and nothing is pacified by the promise of light.
Fragments of cloud unmoor the stars.
Above my bed a familiar face pities
the winter sky, watches the winged
images of a lifetime grope and addle
like wandering bones down the line.
I reach up to touch it, the ritual all
that this night demands, nourished by the
unspeakable bleed of chalk and smoke.
Too old for history or dream, the words
on her lips are hot as fire, cold as ice.

S— 2017

21.

He flaps his arms like a white bird
and flies along the ground in the old
square, collar turned up to the wind.
Black birds settle on tired
statues, not moving, barely visible
under the streetlamps, and lean
against the snow as it covers the world.
He floats between the ground and air.
The trails of his breathing coil dazed
and pale as he sings memories
of superstition and mud, ice binding
his thin shoulders and wrists,
chasing the slow nothing of despair.
The statues kneel, persistent
in the crouch of night, the hollow
wind on eternity's coast the sad
remainder of the day, and beat his
burdens mourning to the ground.
They know together who will die,
the sound of judgment
as it kicks the door that shrives
the world in the chill of the year,
the clamor of the committed charge.
There is no other way home tonight,
no other custom to hallow the street.
This is what the black birds knew.
This is what the black birds know.

22.

I watched from the window
in the eaves of the attic as footprints
scraped the angles of the wild streets
and silence grew, defying gravity,
like a truth gone mad.
Things fall up, not down,
and the bones of the snow keep rising.
It is dangerous here to consider
the shame of the world stripped naked
near the gate, the moment uncapped in
the cold and laid out on a brown mattress
streaked in blood, whose scars are
a roadmap on the slow flanks of
undiscovered countries forever at odds.
The unstable repetition of a final word
I cannot hear below is not enough,
the self a mournful gesture as the city
strikes its own precisions and history
folds to a bag of rags under the stairs.
I never asked to see my future,
never looked this darkness in the eye.
Life is the threshold nothing can re-cross.
I watch the straggler from the house next door
shriek like a bird and fall on his sill.
Silence at last recants its long refrain.
I am caught forever in the shadows
of these rafters, waver north and south
like the needle on the wheel.
I conspire hand in hand with some
wandering god, trip blindly on the edge of time.
The window flakes with a darkening grace,
ignites with the florid moon.

23.

Overhead, the antiphon of the bell
sculpts the air and the final divide
of the quarter hour is a barrier
against the fragile glass. A continuum
of gray houses is lost in a spell
of desperate mirrors, blind-windowed
arches given sight in a blind land.
The heart and mind seek true north,
chiseled in the ice, the patchwork
of the earth meager against their will.
The mark on the palm of your hand
is the incrimination of blood, rough
to the touch, the intent deep in a time
that does not want to come again.
The doors are draped in black,
thresholds sharp as knives and open
to the accusations of the fall.
The solid air thins and broods.
Memory blows hard from the east.
The cold wind trips in its own tracks.

24.

There is a secret hidden in the shapes
of things as they press together like
the fibers of the walls.
The clear forms rise up when the
light goes out, white wings unfurling
in the circles of a dark interior,
beginning again in the vertigo
of a miraculous escape.
It's been a long time now, long past
the memory of it, eyes blind with
the darkness and the snow,
opening and closing, the absence
they feared girding the world.
The night lifts its hand and sets it down,
the sky a dark color it could not imagine,
touching the edges of your skin.
The wind bends pale near the frozen river.
The year turns in its sleep.

25.

An old dog walking alone in the snow
rounds and rounds into a circle
by the base of the statue, its footprints
disappearing as the snow falls and then
uncovering to new ravels unbearable as effigies
of the past combed into their own futures.
Think twice before repeating it, its one
substance melancholy and steady as a swollen eye.
It is an unspeakable arrangement loosing
the black form, a dark scaffold along
the walls of rooms where lovers sleep at odds
and destiny collapses into its own fate.
Give me ignorance, the husk of a trapped
star, make me deaf and blind as a lost dog
in a steady snow, the ecstasy of a world
of sermons and hints wrapped in gray cloths.
Give me blurred glass, the fiery white
of the indecipherable word, the culvert
by the side of the road where the universe
tangles itself to roots and cold water.
Give me at long last the ragged edge of a dream
turned and tense in its own moral point.
Two shapes in the window behind the scaffold
conspire as one, dressed in the skins of angels
or birds, the void fused with its own pardon.
The blind will creates tomorrow out of sullen
abstractions, form and thing invisible as ash
and unstable as the rough stones in the square
that wrest the dog in a confluence of ice.
Night nails its own shadow to a tree.
A cold hand unexpectedly touches my shoulder.
The wind blows.

S. 2014

26.

All these worlds between midnight
and dawn hide in plain sight, stripped
in the flats as the north wind blows.
The eccentricities of the two beginnings
are trapped in mirrors that talk back
to the black voices in the room,
radiant in their twin convulsions.
The yellow eye bends the orbit
of the moon, quick in the pit and dust.
The snow drifts slowly down, here
and along the white shore, as the shadow
gains a foothold by the door.
The prophetic ashes on the floor
have no end, the deep red of the stars
weathered gray as the boards,
and a muddy light fails in the reins.
Something throws the latch, the day
in doubt, and wipes the sleep from its eyes.
Something scatters the hacked horizon,
the thing itself we do not name or control.
Something lifts the stones with white candor,
flying in every direction like unrecorded ghosts.
The forgotten messengers line the dark
cupboards with penciled letters, love for love,
breaking the spokes of the rootless wheel.
There is a sudden cry on the wind, a pausing
of the deepest truths that flakes across the
moon in an ancient shape and sulks against
the hollows of this immaculate stage.
I am alone. The snow presides. The hour delays.

27.

All that remains is a thin line that rises
and falls in the courtyard, an old dog
following at a distance across an eternity
of wind, and the low sound of wheels
dragging to oblivion on a dark horizon.
Their nameless dance in this hour
folds them together in patterns blue
with snow, magnitudes of ice and fire
beyond the tidings of the world.
I listen for a long time, my back
against the empty bedroom wall.
Something whispers in the curtains
that those who confess go free,
drained of protest and resolve
in the undertones of steel.
The covenant of mirror and wind
lays claim to hard semblances
as I reach for the outline of the door.
This city is a bitter glass rimmed with
interruption, fracturing as it twists
and turns across the limits of the universe.
The simple chaos of the lights
below steadies my hand and eye.

28.

I remembered white butterflies
in late spring falling across the
meadows like snow, the history
of the world on hold, and the slow
touch of your hand in the doorway
suddenly close and at ease,
and how you turned and walked away
that last time down the stairs,
across the cobbled street.
These memories come and go
more often now and time takes me
in the darkness by surprise.
I do not want the silences of either.
I watch this winter night curl up
in smoke as God's mystery covers
the far corners of the earth
like snow that falls for a hundred
years on every living thing.
I see your face in each falling seed,
breathe with your breath in the frozen glass.
In the white stillness of this room,
in the final minutes of a sudden dream,
I bear the name that I've been given.

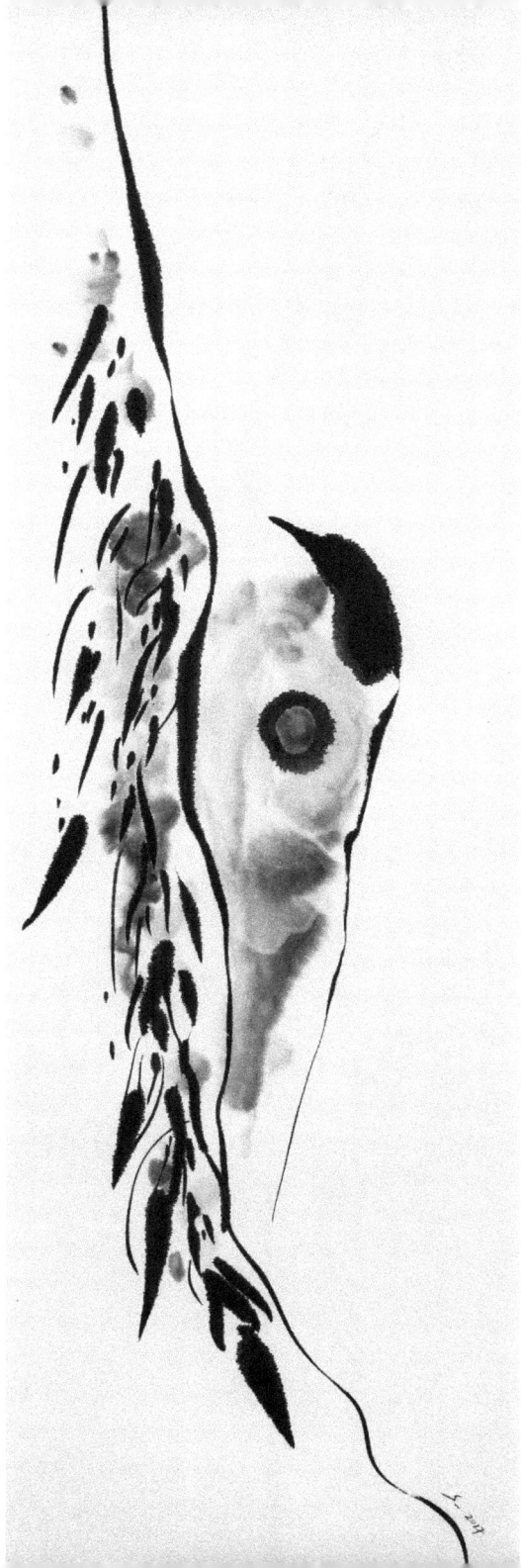

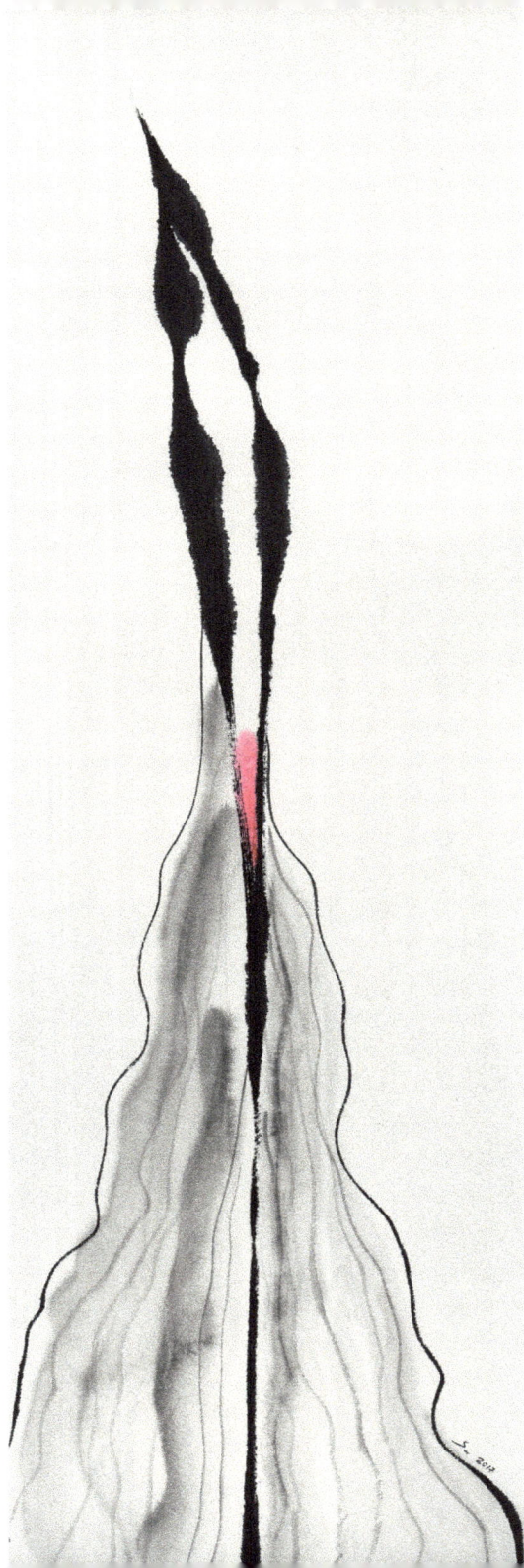

29.

It was a moment I wanted to keep,
the folding history of the north sky
running its course and the sidewalks
cleared and empty at this hour.
Through the window blind an icy light
at the city's end, the secret of how
the world began: centuries of dust,
small things sleeping forever in the cut
of the earth, a dry road leading nowhere,
shattered glass dividing the white of a
single day, a stunned spill and a long fall,
dark stones underground coming up
and out the way a soul might rise
in the invisible wind, in the falling snow.
A white moon beads the clouds,
steady as a circle engraved in glass.
Beyond the square, a train begins
to move again, its slow wheels
husking against their own decay.
The world sinks into its seed.

30.

Up ahead, a few more hours
along the empty road.
The night sky abrupt
as heated metal.
A flock of birds in the distance
rakes the landscape.
An unfamiliar hand brushes
across your back
under a white half moon hanging
in the dark clouds:
a woman in a white dress,
the shake of her voice
as she offers water to the dying,
to you, the dry curtains rustling
as she passes, the smell
of cold air on the line of the horizon
calling her home.
Nothing atones for the coldness
of night, the touch
of her bracelet on your face
the promise of things
you think you know that lifts
the burdens of the ground.
You reach to make the world
your own.
She sits on the bed, resting, waiting,
the sky heavy and close.

31.

And the world is white and white
and white. The city is white with fresh
snow and lightning opens a sky that
presses down on the streets with
the weight of dry bone scrubbed to white
tinder under the ground. The glass
clears as the gates open, wind white
as salt at the beginning of everything
and the end of it all. Bare stones gleam
in a bright light, hundreds of white feathers
covering the strange trees, carrying
the longing that abides and startles
the two shores. Secrets die like a white
candle burning in a dark window, midnight
bending across the horizon like
a blind martyr in a crucible of dreams.
The white flame leaps and dances
across the faces of the brilliant moon.
You turned away from the window, hands
falling, as I stood down below fingers
pressed white against a dangerous ledge.
The red moon hung above the house
like an empty drum, a miniature dimming
sharp-tongued in the square of glass.
The moment ended in self-accusation.
Crows in the narrow yard lifted and shook.

32.

The shadows of hands on the
drawn curtains stretch to pale roses
against the dangerous walls.
Photographs of mothers, daughters,
sisters in black dresses on a table
of dried wood, standing at odds
and misdirection in a cold despair.
The face of a blue child in frozen
water under a bridge that cannot
be kept, remorse for the past
reconciling with the slow crawl of dust
in the corners of the mirror.
The future has no fixed address,
already old when it begins.
The eye of the needle hanging outside
the windows is part of a long epistle,
the last word stitched in old cloth
and unraveling in dark gray light.
The crowded night coughs.
The sky redeems its own abstractions.
In the hallway the secret life of
light and shade scrims a wheel
of breaking glass. The half-moon
in the air cambers the thing affirmed,
the secondary intimations that leave
nothing behind in the newly-fallen
snow, the porcelain that pieces the world
together when night returns.
I pay the ransom in my broad-brimmed
hat, turn my collar up to the angles
and lines that trim the stone bouquet
in the statue's blue hands.
I slip eccentric in an abstract wind,
resolve the last questions of the world.

33.

The opposites in the square lift
to their own corners, breathe in the unison
and repose of the long root.
I think by feeling, each turn a quick splinter
of glass, each flicker of the streetlamp a new
incantation for the dying and the dead.
Secrets endure, naked as a sudden pain
under the ribs, the disorder of a ghostly
voice that wakes in the slow dread
of what it has become, its bitter
conviction incautious at last.
The rest of the night is a dry lift
as God bends down to sweep the stones
in the pavement, appall the summit
of the long dust. It is a world of dreams,
a small place in the trees as I become
branch and wind and the white kingdom
of the river moves into its own vague trace.
That is the last similitude, the last silence
as silence at last subsides, the obscurity
of the self in the darkness of the day.
Nothing comes here to stay, nothing grates
from door to door as the summit swells
to a time that seeps through my veins,
nothing tangles the miraculous escape.
It is more like a downward progression
along the meridians of the world,
the salience of marrow and stone
in a center filled with centers,
each meaning bearing a differing weight.
The great night stands still, the agency
of the flesh rising before the great fall.
The moment gathers. The wind broods.

34.

The slats of the window hide all
that is innocent, all that is lost or forsaken
in the random currents of truth tonight.
The crouch of the walls is a white embrace,
a struggle to lift from this place without
a single beat of a wing under the streetlamps,
pierce the clouds above the crows' cries,
feel the hard slam of iron and steel
as the doors below close.
It is all chaos, I know that now, some
random impaling of the light, not
a predicted effect or certain analogy
of action but a congress of limps
and desires unmet when the thin bones
ride the loosed horses.
I need nothing more, I have no need
to know why, no need to understand
the articulations that divide us:
it is the nothing from
which the same new beginnings come,
equally unsteady in a shifting wind,
that veers too close when the ice
unexpectedly turns to flame, when
I pin my shadow to the wriggling moon.
Light tonight is the infinite ash that covers
the floor, all that remains of the stars
when eternity coughs itself out and bleeds.

35.

A procession of streetlamps circles
the statues and horses below, the lost world
crossing its own numbers and letters out.
Their light filters through falling snow,
summoning the sky as it hollows to silence
in the west, the effigies of history thrust
in my hands like a moment of crisis.
How foolish it is to dream, to cross
the planes between these worlds:
you turn and tell me you are caught
in the chair and cannot move across
the room to me, your blouse lifting
like morning on your back.
This room is heavy with the past,
you transparent in this momentary place.
The curious lie persists.
The world is neither black nor white.
The wind continues on its way, pushing
the strangers on their long walk home.

36.

Chance events and the chaos of birds
in a distant light mark your return
home on the first day after the
shadows of a hard winter's sleep.
Wires on poles along the street
sag with the remains of snow.
Hands scratch and hide
in old pockets, fingers grieving
with the indifference of white faces.
Strangers on corners and steps
are imitations of the double thread,
the harsh quick as morning nears,
destiny a dark harbor and endless maze.
God himself has already come and gone,
a trick of light in the shaking air.
The old woman passing by the lost
angels drags the night into a vacant lot.
The mind is caught in the bonds
of its own making, indelible and restless
as the deep tides swell.
In the half-empty room, as the sky
grows black and red, something
knocks against the cold door.
A white-colored man in white
clothing rides past on a white horse.

37.

They lead the white horse
at midnight between the fence
posts and rails, watching which
of its legs, right foot or left, steps
first in the furrows of each marked row,
its halting movements across
the stones a conjuring or divination.
The earth blackens and splits
like a dry seed as the gate slams shut,
the land infertile on the horizon,
and the snow drifts down
to a burial of cold smoke.
I never wanted to see that place,
branching into hard lines
that beat across the street,
the future a single hour under
a dark November sky squared
to a sunken thing under the stairs.
There, the consolations of truth in
ambiguous circles leave no tracks
and silence deepens by degrees,
brittle variables of a temporal mind.
There, the moment before the storm
falls away invisible and time braids
together mystery and faith. There.
The clock unexpectedly strikes three.
The horse in the distance
in the dark by the fence winces
with snow then bites the air.

38.

The moment stretches and breaks
as shadows from the lone lamp
on the corner fall across the sudden points
of the street, unnamed glass and steel
reflecting the last hope of a dry return.
An erratic life scrapes by in counter-
currents on the other side of the light,
the equilibrium of the world balanced
in the symmetry edged between midnight
and the back alleys of dawn, the doors
that never open shaken by a rising wind.
The house at this hour is a dead echo,
the absolute of night's black space.
The mirror on the deep wall reflects
a face that night has turned to stone,
the arc of the moon tracing the end
of everything, the peripheries and centers,
far past the outlines of the half-dark room.
The pieces of the world sleep for a hundred
years tonight with the ghosts on the corner,
the drift of time churning to thin smoke
and the colloquies of dreams.
The restless stars bristle above the road,
falling with the weight of white feathers, and
the noises below list against the last low wall.
In the patience of this moment, in the
loneliest of all my days, I am the secret name
that brings the house down to a drawn
conclusion, the perilous silence
the air yields to in a dimming light.

39.

One circle of bare ground by the gate catches
the flame and snow angles the face of the moon.
Nothing is neglected as the passageways recede,
existence a consolation of a single truth and a
difficult peace in the imbalance of both hands.
I try to keep my mind on other things: the train
at the edge of the city, a sudden pale shaft of light,
the way the future and past cancel the senses,
a quickened pulse on the changing landscape,
and the pity of iron that cuts the surface
of steel as rail cars seep slowly into the station.
I regret that I can't ride them in this signal hour,
regret the erratic wagging of the road ahead.
I stand instead on one leg, head back and arms
extended, turned against the wall, the outlines
of the earth capped in redemption on my head.
The energy of the world is contained in forms
that open again to fill the dialectical void.
Life darts for cover as winter birds sing with
the knowledge that things are as they are and
always will be, that the loose black boards
of the world will forever hollow in their wake
as stars explode to the shapes of red glass.
Fear answers fear in a long pursuit, and in the
interchange around me I see the gate's ajar.

40.

I trace my finger through the dust on the
floor, death an orphan in these motions.
The patterns my fingers make are a
sanctuary of artificial lines, the clarity
and wholeness of existence held fast
in their own source, nothing distorted,
the certainties I draw a self-accusation
whose end or meaning I will not know.
Reconciliation is familiar as a scar.
The hour arrives: the hand of God
traces its fingers across my face,
gropes across the harsh walls of the hall,
and then moves on, deaf and blind,
into a cascade of flame and cold snow.
I sketch my life like a long cloak
on the floor, inundations of the universe
that break the light of the eye,
the marks of those fingers on my face
part of the world I inhabit alone.
And then the hour passes: the splendor
of the flying world gathers in the dust.
The shades of heaven fumble on the floor.

41.

The day must be given a different ending,
white and long on the rooftops, as we hasten on.
The lost birds feed on flowers rooted in ice,
trapped in anonymous gardens where silence
gathers under cupolas of snow and fog settles
in the proportions of its own destination.
The body can come to life again, can remember
an innocent love in another garden, the brief light
of summer calm in the calligraphy of leaf and vine,
constant in the interventions of the rose.
We remain there forever, as forms of light,
even as night falls and falls in this flat land.
There is no limit on desire, no truth that
will unredeem the flesh, no sound
that will unwind the fidelity of our voices.
The end already exists and we sleep so soon.
The one truth I know cuts across the air.
Let me be blind once more in the bright yard,
let my heart cry out in joy, in the street below,
for the kind salvation of a faint blue light.

42.

I did not expect to see him through
the interruptions of the gray window:
the odd little man dressed in green
and black turning around in the street
at every third step to count the footprints
he had left behind in the snow, up again
to the yellow stairs that lead to his door:
one foot the frame of a well-worn boot,
the other the foot of a hobbled bird.
He stops and starts like a cold ember, knows
that the clawed foot drags the plow of time,
scratching the earth as it scuttles the west
and paling in the migrant orbits of stars.
He knows that if the burning eye that hangs
above him in the square falls across the sky,
shadows will hollow the walls he stumbles
against, elide the red ash on the doorsills
he hops across on one leg unaware.
He knows the vellum and the flicker,
the involuntary rule that flutters in the charge,
and the woman he has not yet named who
sleeps undone in the bottle and the sash.
His shadow is itself a shadow of a shadow.
His nervous hand still prods the air.
His feet again are cold.
I turn off the lantern in the window
he so watches, lid the burning eye.

43.

I have begun to live in memory,
lay yellowed photographs out across
the kitchen table, read old love letters
saved in bent brown folders, try to
find familiar stars in lost constellations.
It's hard at the outset to break
the boundary, to reach for shapes
that fill the space made by a moving hand,
to hold what can be held and then
let go and float free in a beam of light.
Truth is harmless in November.
The only epoch is my own.
I am a strange face in the mirror,
the sudden recollection of a forgotten place,
dull with loss and perplexed by the glare.
I am tonight the color of wind in a
headland of rocks that binds the old moon,
the world retrieved through a glass darkly
and piled in stacks on a table of wood.
The ellipse of the past folds a universe
of balance and risk into a savage now.
The present drives the moment
to the wildness of snow, time gone
and to come spinning on its axis.
The landscape's face is ice and stone.

44.

She tells me that she sometimes dreams
of going mad. Her voice is every shade
of red, the synthesis and symbol of an old
place under an old and darkening sky.
The night each night howls and sighs as she
trembles with the echoes of her walk.
Her fingers tap the moon in the mirror
on its dark gray brow, desire awkward
in its slide, and the dull knife cuts the last
shapes of white paper, the masters of time.
The table moves under her, swings back in the
dark, a gateway to the sounds this winter mocks.
Every shadow on the street and walls folds to a
new myth freed from the innocence of the past.
This is the prophecy of hope in the attic,
the muddled ghost of our love, that waits
for us out there like the certainty we seek.
She presses herself against the wall,
her voice constantly changing its hues,
and complains about the cold, the night.

45.

I move. Far from the river,
the night dies well.
She moves. Far from the city,
bleak land rebels.
We move. Far from the statues,
broken glass swells.
They move. Far from the windows,
wind robs the bell.
All this is part of a careful layer
that haunts my memories,
defiant and thin-skinned as a prayer,
sinking the undertones of centuries
of wrought iron and the frozen courage
of that other age.
It was the time of glass
when I was glass,
consuming the light of the world
and never reflecting it back.
The conviction of the spectrum
divides the colors of the world
and the life to come.
All tonight are gray and black.

S~ 2017

46.

Night hovers between two moons,
rises and falls between two horizons.
On the wall, the hands of the clock
synchronize to a steady habit,
the hour striking three, and the self
bears its own reassurance against
the arch of the sky. The past peels
like a paper wrapper in my hands.
We knew we could live forever
in the long pursuit of color and form,
would not allow ourselves
to be easily found, the tides of summer
and winter buried in time together and
waking only briefly and against their will
in rituals that shorten or lengthen
the night. Each was the first day
of seeing, the world ours for the taking,
as the sky expanded and receded.
Each a push and pull against a horizon
that lies steady on the horizon and does
not accept whatever we had of grace.
The pattern endures, pained by its own
weight at the stubborn edge of fall.
The root of the future is an insolent
myth as it stumbles down the stairs
and deadbolts the door.

47.

There are no objects in the world,
no things trapped by chance events,
that run across the world dressed
in the hides of white horses.
They stride in an imagined place,
witness to what the darkness
of the latticework on the balcony did.
The cells divide, ice into ice,
everything closing one by one
in the blunting of the night.
Why do we forget so soon,
hide ourselves among the lost bags
on the train and see the motion
of the hand that strikes us down?
It hangs heavy from the ceiling,
rises darkly from the floor,
scrapes and scratches through
the wall smoldering to the west.
You drink the wine as blood
anoints your head, the mercy of
God's face in the ice too terrible to see.
No need to bring it up.
Pretend you never heard.
Strip the gains of that other world that
peel back the invisible shores of a lost
city tethered to the snow as it falls.
The blind man rambles through
the house, still searching for the stairs
he cannot find though he knows
they lead nowhere.

48.

It was a temporary covenant of rooftops
gone astray as the streets drifted
to the underline the river made
just past the corners of the square,
binding fast the thresholds of the hour.
Small and sure, the dark rider sits
outside the window, the endless
whispers of a forgotten saint troubling
the bewilderment of her mistakes.
Her life is not only her own,
not just some metaphysical fable
or parable of snow that misdirects
the iconography of the world.
She is the word that resonates
on the other side of thinking,
the surface and the substance
of the idea and of the thing
that sift the earth as the houses
all around me shake and rise,
atonement and redemption
hidden in the threaded grain.
The past is cold and naked
in the window, time a bag
of bones shaken in the street.
Night drags the four shadows
up the stairs, knocking at the door,
and something invisible burns.
She closes her eyes and pays
no mind, the half-moon chalked
in a mist that dims in the mirror.
We can no longer falter on, casting
pale reflections in the darknesses
we wander, we can no longer harden
the world to perplexity and hide
in a sleep that flickers like death

against the spill of the night.
The river tallies the outlines of
tomorrow, sounds across the
incriminations of ice in the square.
She keeps her eyes on other things,
forgives the truth that can't be told.
A key turns quietly in the lock.

49.

The counterpoint to grace leads to a cave
that roots in a deep distortion.
Fire curls like water at every turn and stains
the snow in the square, the web cast and
ours for the taking as night overwhelms the sky.
The bodies of the world hover on winter air
blowing in a narrow wind like loose banners
or carved patterns shaped by heaven's sterile eye.
If he were living now, words heavy as prose,
he would walk the streets forever and bring
the wrecker's ball down on all the shuttered
houses of our lives. Life would no longer
be a culling of all that will die in all the towns
we may have seen, a harmless dream where
the trees have all fallen and the heart has bled.
We still hope for the world not to withdraw
to the point of faith, to coil like a reformation
of the past growing in a long dark line.
I push against the cold damp walls
of this place, outlined by no rules and
modulating this hard pursuit, and time seeps
away slowly to a desolate mark.

50.

Cold numbs my fingers as I scratch
the frozen light from the edges
of the window, my breath
congealing on the sibilant glass.
The church tower in the shadows
that lap the street is dark as the day
of judgment, dark as the day when
ghosts whose names I tap on the glass
will reclaim the borders of the world.
We pretend there's time to change sides,
carve new images in the ice
and turn the index over in a flat land
where tomorrow, poised on the
threshold, looks in and out,
a narrow orbit swallowing time whole.
Stillness moves into stillness,
repeats itself with no consolation.
The streets are empty and the hour dead.
I am transparent in the window,
float measureless on a mortal scale,
my face and its reflection
a random synthesis that struggles
in history and granite, not sure
which fragile patterns to choose
as the sky looks coldly down.
I hide under the covered table, the
ranks of black boxes precisely aligned.
The room recedes neglected down
the stairs and I make myself small
in a stirring of musty air.
A blade of light pierces my heel.

51.

The water in the river in the center
of the city moves the way all dark waters
move under the ice, the stitch of the last
cold wall a fierce barrier on the horizon
fixed in the middle of things as snow
compounds the ratios of night.
Dressed in black and kneeling
at the end of the bridge, she raises
a divining eye across the banks and the
course of the world creaks and turns.
The stars begin to shine, the meaning
of the moment bleeding to white.
The burials of a thousand years go up
in smoke, wet wood burning in chimneys
and rising on slow flanks of wind and air.
She counts out the flames, the will of heaven
answering nothing in the reflections
of ice among the pilings and rafters.
She balances the soul's fall in the
monotony of insufficient gods, measures
the depths of the forms of the river
and the shapes of the ideas of time.
She sighs with the syllables of my name,
with the memory that keeps them there,
pushing away the white face of the moon.
The shell separates the water and ice,
charting the defiance of a lost equilibrium.
The clock on the wall strikes three.

52.

In the middle of the world,
on a stone bench, near the row
of seven houses whose doors
are perpetually closed, an old
love letter half-covered with snow
lies left behind by a tired hand,
the landmark of a dark interior
where drawn shades fall
to a broken disguise.
The dim eyes of statues
watch the snow fall, filling
the empty streets beyond the green
shutters of borrowed rooms.
The dead weights of all
the clocks in all the houses
struggle toward the black
façade of time, lights fading
in attics like a split moon.
The hand dreams of a
forgotten name inscribed
on the envelope in red ink,
the awkward intrusion of silence
through a black-draped window
indecorous with ribbons and dust.
The past is a stray draft on
a bare floor, some pages blank.
Darkness scatters to darkness.
A small door stands open, near
the tower, to the restless wild
singing of this winter's night.

53.

I don't know exactly how long it
was suspended like a pillar of salt
in the spun glass of the city, moving
back and forth with the sound a moment
makes as it breaks against a marble wall.
It touches the ground quickly then lifts up
just as fast, indecent in its suppositions
of redemption, light and dark as
a heavier stone rolled forever up a hill.
I remember when the sea began,
when the landscape opened itself
to let the waters in, how the moon lies
down under the bridge, never living long
enough to paint the faces of angels.
Somewhere in the history of the world
an aging man stumbles in the street
and understands all the things
he will never be able to do or say.
Time, as always, ebbs and flows
to a sway of memory and illusion.
He walks alone, tapping his stick
against the walls, emerging like a single
cry along the margins of the square.
Shadows perched on the statues there are
the only living presence in the widening arc.

54.

The hand knows what it wants to touch:
a world of glass, brittle and transparent,
history folded to an effigy hung
on the gray stones of an anonymous square.
The awkward wind below turns on itself,
an intruder of salt and cold that divides its
own meanings in the judgments of the moon.
In the private light of this room I hobble
on wings of wax and feathers, rise invisible
as gray smoke against the arched high ceiling,
burn like tinder in the angel's eye, virtuous
to the last. I reverse the shadows of the reticent
world, contradict the uncommon nature
of the angled street as a sky white with snow
retracts to the antithesis of its own beginning.
I know there has been a serious mistake:
this night is black as this day and this day white
as this night. Time falls to the inverse colloquy
of color, its patterns precise on the frozen floor.
It is the salient movement of the wheel.
So let me be sharp and blind as glass,
reflecting and absorbing a place where
nothing seems to end, the negative of light.
Let me float through the windows, prowl
the dark corners as the night withdraws,
nameless as the faces in the clouds.
I feel suddenly uneasy about myself, know
this room is not a hippodrome or stage,
and make a simple statement of fact:
all this nonsense about the living
and the dead, these opposites that
affirm the world, is a dream
that each dreams of the other.
I am perfectly safe from the snow
and the horses in this room tonight.

If anything exists, let it drop like a hand
against the implacable walls,
let it unchain itself and gallop through
the black streets savage and wild.
The air glistens with slivers of glass.
No news ventures about tomorrow.

55.

The year has its rituals, silent and blind,
and the undercurrents echo from every wall.
We pity ourselves with a gesture we cannot
reach, a circle where light fades and an
unfamiliar god descends, cropping the horses.
The second error flays the mist, the shaken
dust passing like a breath on winter air,
counterpoint and dominant restored.
He is suddenly gone among the gray flames,
disappearing around the corner in a private
pace as the doors close. The force of gravity
is different tonight, time no longer counts.
A hand pushes through the snow,
moving in and out, then snaps the last rein.
Everything hangs upside down on a single word.

56.

The moment that follows each moment
is a snare of no use to anyone,
the nothing that comes after each nothing.
I dreamed last night that I would dream
last night that night fell cold through the closed
window into my room and the wilderness out
beyond the river at the edge of the square made
its way back to another bend of the river outside
the closed window of my room near the square.
These images remain and grow upside
down like dead seeds sprouting on the ledge
of the pantry window waiting for the world
to turn upside down again, a mirror likeness
of itself on a horizon that cannot open, and
blossom into horses' hooves grounded in mid-air.
Tomorrow, in my dream of tomorrow
I will send a letter to myself, the end
not written, no signature composed.
I hope to be surprised to see what it comes to
in the end, whose name will close the closing line.
Or I'll contemplate the movements of stones,
the contradictions that tie nature and art together
into simpler compulsions, as I shift in my bed
contemplating the slow movements
and contradictions of stones in my bed.
The season of decay is kept from decay.
In the bright night the dark is too deep.
We can argue either side from either side.

57.

The pigeons sleep on the storm gutters
along the ragged line of the roof and nothing
assuages the odd shadows in the square.
The metal stairs turn away from the brick walls
and wind catches asterisks of cinders and lights
that twist in the windows to a certain demise.
The stirring of the birds as the air streaks
to gray ends the distractions of mortality.
The only end to be found pauses as the wind
unwinds and shuts its eyes so it will not die alone.
Fire comes out of the horizon, low in the offing,
the hour brief. Blood lingers in the utterances
of birds, and the dead will not unbend
the last white star. Footsteps in the hallway
pace and drop, a white glove crumbling
clods of dirt to the outline of an absent dress.
A solitary crow sits on a telephone wire
and a silent wheel revolves in the sky
like an answered prayer in a reticent night.
Black keys unlock the hanging box.

58.

The troubled pacing of infinity on the edge
of an insubstantial light is a half-whisper
of fire that slowly burns itself out.
Night is slow to pass, both absent and
present, known and unknown, caught
in a time that lurks outside of time.
There is no new storm coming, the small
space between midnight and dawn
in which I have lived is fixed forever
in these colors and forms, the horizon
under the eaves weightless with a flutter of
birds against the white of the universe.
Morning smolders around a long corner.
Ice breaks like a conversion of smoke.
I reach for the touch of glass and stone
as I pass by the fountain.
The white horses mount the stage,
spin illuminated at the center and the edge,
splintering the horizon like a shriveled stick.
The empty mirror of the sky opens like
a tragic stare and the darkness of the world's
undone by a gathering light.

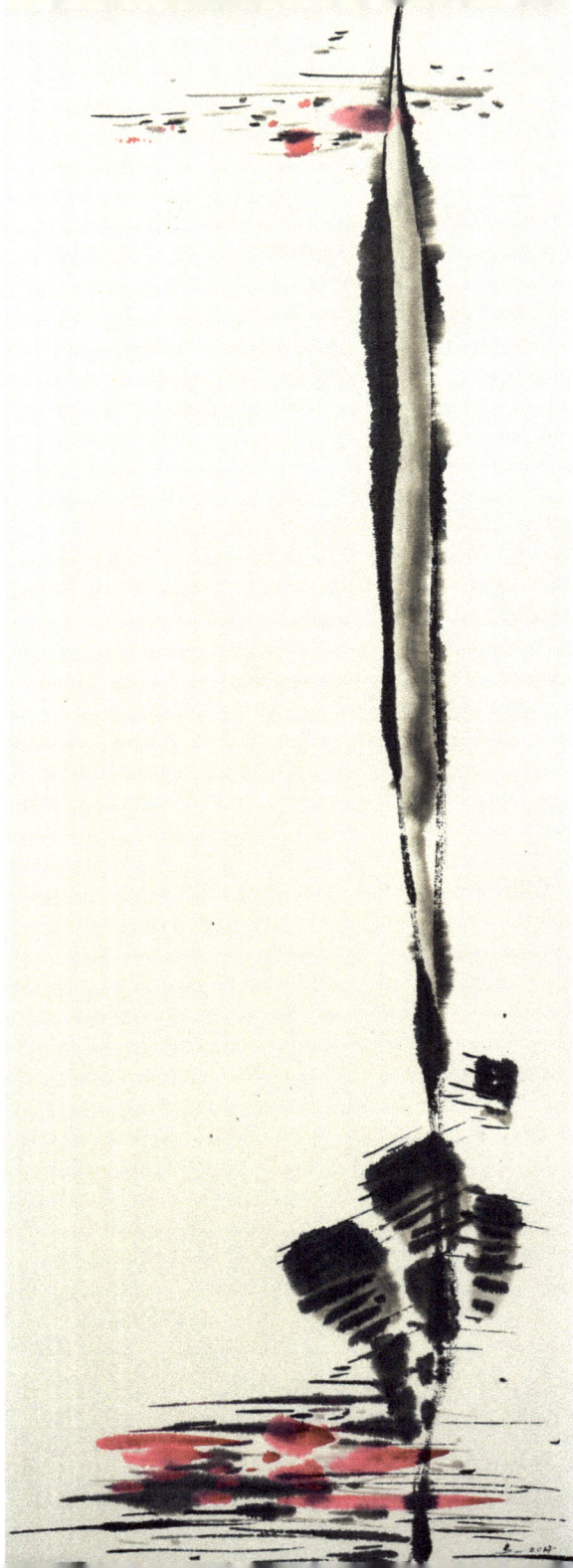

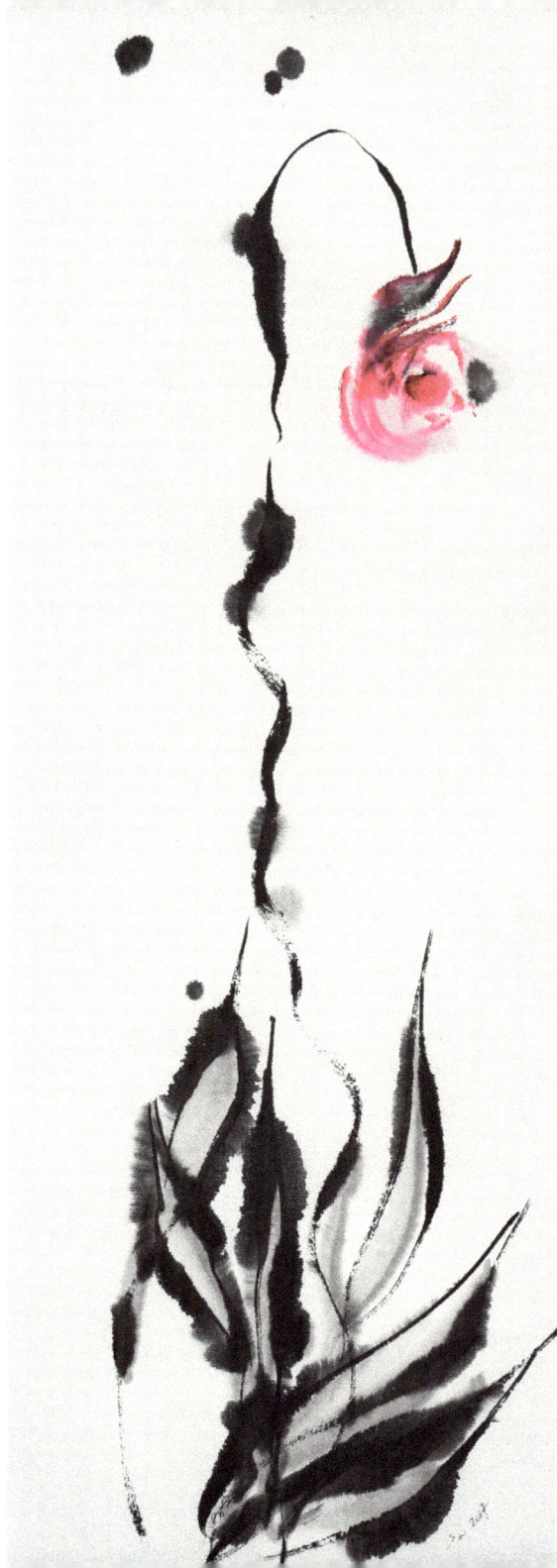

59.

I did not find them again and could not admit
that they were lost, the lamps exhausted
in the dead weight of a moment that would not
intercept the light. The statues outside moved
across the square with a loose familiarity,
the wind bowing on the door sills, heavy-footed
and alone against the involuntary grains
of a sky arching from the dark stems of a thousand
nights and the hard paradigms of drift and snow.
The hours of early morning, when the journey
still leads them around blind corners, muffle
the stars that turn among the thinning clouds
and strum the hard walls of a hundred rooms.
Winter will begin and winter will end,
in this country and in that other, and the heart
will break to clarity in the visions of that light.
The chaos of renewal where the lost are found
runs four-footed through the streets, and the
coming day, as it scrapes the roofs, revises
its blank stare, the lamps on the corner faltering off.

60.

Life will sing its lines in the branches
of old trees and in the deep roots, scratching
breathless down the streets, and the earth
will rise to vapor and air beneath my feet.
A shallow light on a winter's day
will hone the buildings and these walls,
shape the balance of the blowing wind
and the ceremonies of white curtains.
The birds on the wires will dance
their secrets, will stir their wings toward
the dry streak of red on the horizon,
and the horses framed in the solitude
of the square will shake the tangled snow
from their backs, the prefigured possibilities
of time and space the brilliant chord
that will tune the illusions of the world.
The clock in the distance strikes six.
The black and the white release
the shadows in the hallway underfoot.
I push back the flow of the seasons, write
my name on the brightening glass,
carve the dangerous wisdoms that offend
the world on the green wall, and morning,
rising on the long screen of heaven, wanders
and strays to an eternal image in the mist.

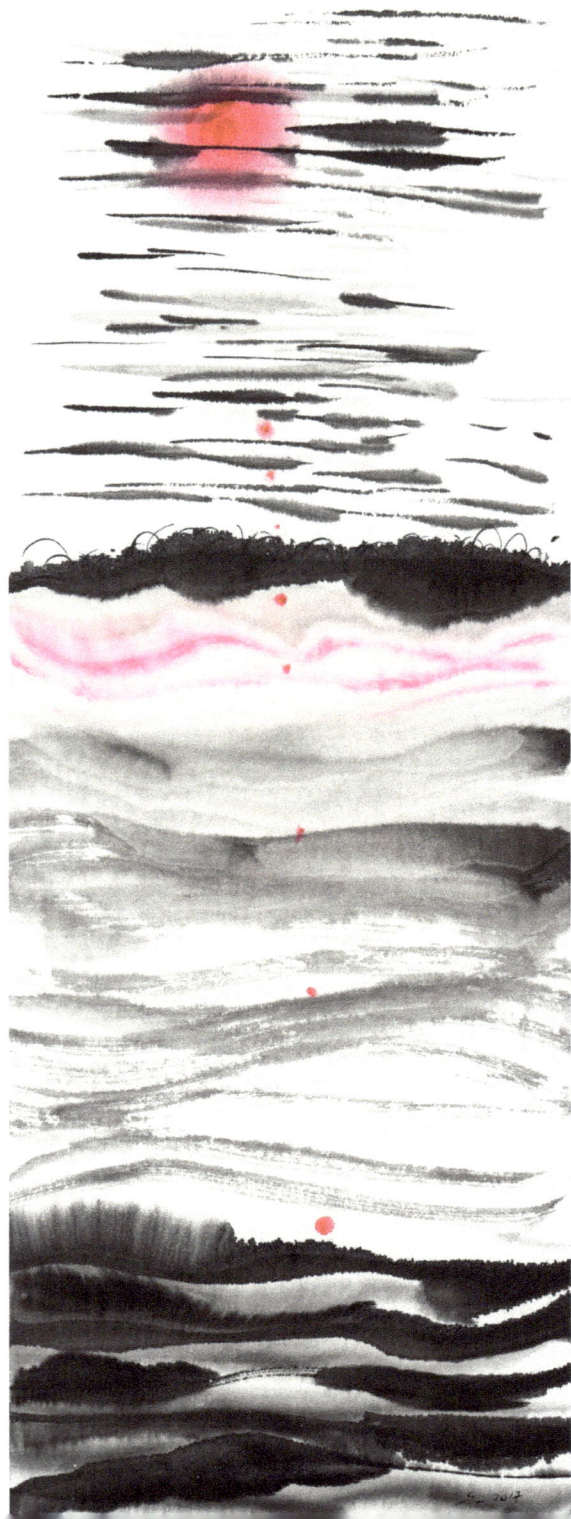

61.

The year goes its own way,
witness to the indecisions of the sky,
and moves time out of the dark
cupboards of the world in winter.
The promise is kept in the hulls
of the sky, borne on the wings
of black crows and opening like an
unexpected dream of a woman
I do not have in a room I cannot enter.
Truth is a congregation of faces
reflected in the window leaving
as they enter, trembling hands
holding an unburied stone.
The grace of intention reaches the edge,
papers blown by wind in the streets
honing the likeness of whitening ground.
The three bronze horses in the square
turn toward the denominations of day.
The beginning of everything, fixed in the
fall of these things, lifts in its own end.

62.

It's not enough to want to come
into the light, to separate from darkness,
to reveal that aspiration, hidden deep,
to choose the absolute over the original
revelation and weather a harmless truth
that sits still and silent at an empty core.
The end of the year again like the year
before, and I catch my breath.
I fix my attention on the stitches
in the curtain, take whatever cold that comes.
I remember how I complained about
the stairs, the blown glass hanging dark
above the bannister, the idea
of the permanence of light loose
and half ready in a transient light
that wastes itself like an imagined moon
hanging in a noose of dark clouds and wind.
I like the order of that, the consequences
of the pentads and decahedrons of glass
as the universe inches to renewal,
burned by a distant source and struck
to the small fractures of lost afternoons.
The streets unravel, pluck the taut strings
that bind the edges of the dominion of air:
the narrows of a second sight that limits
the white chaos of the sky, the end unwritten.
The slow cold wind sighs.
The bones in my hand, as I lift them
to the possibility of light in the window,
under pale skin are hard and white.

63.

I weigh the results of the world on scales
of fire and ice, my eye fast on traveling water.
I make my way across the old stones of the
square, an awkward parody of myself, seek
the solace of things that angle in the dark.
A streetlamp illuminates another view,
transfixing the horses. Their vacant eyes
sleep in the mausoleum of the city's heat.
In this blank limit we are all frail creatures, wary
and ill-at-ease under the arches, tenuous in our
petitions to the brief dignities of the world.
We are drawn to our own separations,
unaware of the brilliance to come and the
dispensations of migrating birds.
On hands and knees I mark the middle
of the fall of things, the integer of lost horizons,
fingers digging for the hidden faults of stones.
And what is protected here now?
What did you see before darkness covered it all?
What stories did you tell in the exile of this life?
The night stirs toward another year,
the ground swelling to a bronze shape
that no repetition can prolong. The sound
of water under ice is a last resort,
long done, of the covenant and seal.
The steady drone in the windows of fading
voices is the only truth I know. Snow hones
the statues and walls, compounds
the margins as they grow opaque.
The corona of the moon drags along the streets
like a dark stalk, stars hung in effigy overhead,
and the balance in my hands splays the bare poles.
In the language of the silent mirror,
I reach the two conclusions, spin the world
to chaos for the timid and the mad.
The balance rotates on my hand as
the stones in the pavement fall and rise.

64.

The only light is a small cluster
of stars and a thin crescent
of the moon that hangs across
an old red roof thick with the
gestures and truths of night.
The strange thing rings hollow
in the annulments of this season,
the black edge of an ancient reward
tacked empty in the gray glide.
The world unrolls like a ball
of wet string through cold fingers,
the path of death in brief stars,
and the last blue light of the past unveils
itself in the loose boards of the floor.
Seven black crows tangle the ice
of the river, the mysteries of their
sidelong dance with the shadows
in the snow exhausting the void.

65.

The horse reflected on the wall lowers its head,
lifts its left front hoof as snow piles on the sill.
The limits of the world are hard and blank.
Overturned jars on the shelves in the pantry,
illuminated by candles trembling in the wake
of coarse red curtains, have been empty for years,
the periphery and center of the bones of dried
insects and birds. Old papers and used books
fill the corners of the room, the moment passing
above them a small defect of light. The man
kneeling on the linoleum tiles crosses himself,
turns his head to the shadows in the hall.
He hears the sounds of clouds falling into deep
holes, sees the woman standing alone near the high
ceiling hurrying nowhere, feels her white hand
write in chalk and fire on the cold black wall.
The signs she makes call them to the light.
They rise in a circle in the snow-dusted square,
stand without moving under an opening sky.
The horse lifts its leg and lowers its head.

66.

All who pass by lose their way
in the streets, all who climb the stairs
contemplate the burials of friends.
The cold smoke of my breath folds
across the window panes, outlining
the shapes of old words scrawled
on the glass in a language I can't recall.
Perhaps the knife did not go deep
enough, its blue sound an elaborate
confusion that swaddles the walls
and cumbers our necessities.
Free will rebukes this world, the end
clear, and the ungovernable fear hangs
its head in expectation, its flat boxes
stacked in the hallway under the stairs.
Something stares with white eyes from
the corner of my bed, something wheedles
the old woman nodding in the fire.
I sleep and wake at every hour, sidle
in the present and the past, each of my
faces whispering to each other, each
reflected in the clouding glass.

67.

The black shoals of air along the river
narrow under a green bridge gray with rust.
There is no entrance, no exit in the ice,
nothing that muffles the stir of morning.
The left bank is clear, the rocks
of the right covered in algae and snow.
The stems of the winter weeds
are marked with invisible wounds.
The abstraction of form falls to
the vacant stare of brown water.
Nothing slows, no wall holds it back.
Something shifts, a sudden breaking, slopes
the venerations of birds in dark branches.
The air is marginal in its usual grief,
unwinding to another kind of death.
The wind counts its fingers, crows leap and dive.
I'm not there, I'm here. I listen, I talk.
I see myself out to a world without end.

68.

I whistle for the silence of another morning,
dance and chant in ceremonies of ice and stone
as stars fracture like pieces of colored glass
burning back and forth in ancient ceramic.
Cold fills the curtains as I open the window.
The ledge piles up and the wind is loud,
recognitions stale in the fade of night
and defiant as a rising shout.
The watchman passes in the street below
checking the doors, the consent and failure
of the green lights of a world restored, but
never looks up, never watches me watching.
The wall on the other side of the square still
stands, indistinguishable from the snow,
a confluence of forms that rebukes the dark river.
I want to be lifted up and out the window of this
place, float like a mysterious bird on a white
horizon, forever avoiding the hard wisdom of
the grave, hurrying down before the shadow returns.
It will be the only bright thing I ever do,
the sky growing pale and blue, home once more.
Or if I step out of my body, into a separate
silence, I may become whatever it is the snow
becomes as it melts and rises, whatever it is the wind
absorbs on its naked slide across the last square.
I open the window, and myself, to find it.

69.

The writing on the wall, the signs
on the window, the marks on the floor
are still as crystal in a changing light.
After she was gone, I closed up the room,
imagining the dust on the brown rafters
falling like snow in a field of stars.
The emblems of the last post in the dead
street are a call to reason and grief.
Old men husk the seed that splits the world,
brooding in dark corners and trunks,
and think about the eternal silence of the day.
It rides along an ancient road, bumping
like a broom into every door, and rapt
like a final word carved in dark wood.
I do not want to wander any more,
will not surrender as the candelabrum
scales the rust that streaks the bridge and
dark birds fly in awkward patterns upstream
against a cold current we will not bear.
I am spirit and flesh on a hard winter's day.
I move over and under the ice.

70.

A world of white, the perfect
harvest of snow and light that
spreads across the scrawls
of love in the distance,
fears the cold progeny of ice
that mantles the outskirts of town.
Something stands on its own
in the mist, the sleep of the
landscape the exception to the
rule as trees interleave with
vapors and roofs.
It looks for something, the certainty
of time or the views of the end
that the wind blows back
to their own beginnings.
The slow perception that names
the composition of the glass
rounds the screen and leans
against the drying wind.
These small moments keep their
high resolve, the one meaning
balanced on the obstinate bridge.
It will not fall.
It will not pale in the hundred
years of snow that stray
to unanimous consent.
It will not hide in past tense.
And the moment comes,
and we cross the hour,
and we run across the blue
horizon, the sky and earth
a single billow in white curtains.
And my life opens like a seed,
dances in two like the
anonymous saint who winds

the clock in the last tower.
The great room turns on its wing.
I touch the door to the watching hall.